My Day at the
BEACH

Jory Randall

PowerKiDS press™

New York

Published in 2010 by The Rosen Publishing Group, Inc.
29 East 21st Street, New York, NY 10010

First Edition

Editor: Joanne Randolph
Book Design: Julio Gil
Photo Researcher: Jessica Gerweck

Photo Credits: Cover, pp. 5, 9, 11, 13, 15, 19, 21, 24 (top left, bottom right) Shutterstock.com; pp. 7, 24 (bottom left) Uwe Krejci/Getty Images; p. 17 Jose Luis Pelaez/Getty Images; p. 23 Robert Warren/Getty Images; p. 24 (top right) www.iStockphoto.com/Cheryl Casey.

Library of Congress Cataloging-in-Publication Data

Randall, Jory.
   My day at the beach / Jory Randall. — 1st ed.
      p. cm. — (A kid's life)
   Includes index.
   ISBN 978-1-4042-8074-8 (library binding) — ISBN 978-1-4358-2467-6 (pbk.)
ISBN 978-1-4358-2468-3 (6-pack)
   1. Beaches—Juvenile literature. I. Title.
   GB453.R36 2010
   796.5'3—dc22
                                      2008051373

Contents

We love to go to the beach with our family for the day. The beach is so much fun!

5

I always wear **sunblock** at the beach. Sunblock keeps my skin safe from the sun.

We dig in the sand at the beach. We build **sandcastles** with all the sand we dig.

We can build a **tunnel** in the sand, too. Be careful of the sides!

My brother and I look for shells on the sand. What do you like to do at the beach?

I found a **crab** at the beach. I need to be very careful so that I do not hurt the crab.

Playing games at the beach with friends is fun, too. We are playing tug-of-war.

Time to go in the water! Swimming at the beach is fun and it keeps me cool.

My dad and I stand in the water close to the shore. We look for starfish and small fish.

It's time to go home. I hope we come to the beach again soon.

Words to Know

crab

sandcastle

sunblock

tunnel

Index

Web Sites

Due to the changing nature of Internet links, PowerKids Press has developed an online list of Web sites related to the subject of this book. This site is updated regularly. Please use this link to access the list:
www.powerkidslinks.com/kidlife/beach/